12 ROUNDS WITH
OSCAR
DE LA HOYA

An Illustrated Tribute to Boxing's Brightest Star

Published by: Beckett Publications

15850 Dallas Parkway Dallas, TX 75248

ISBN: 1-887432-50-7

Cover photo by Blake Little / Sygma

12 Rounds with Oscar De La Hoya is not licensed, authorized or endorsed

by any league, boxing organization or Top Rank Boxing,

nor is it authorized or endorsed by Oscar De La Hoya.

First Edition: October 1998

Corporate Sales and Information (972) 991-6657

CONTENTS

INSIDE THE RING

Whenever he has chosen to venture into the ring, Oscar De La Hoya unquestionably has proven himself a winner. From his amateur success to the undeniable impact of his early pro career, he's been trained by the best to beat the best. That's why many consider him to be, pound-for-pound, the best fighter in the game today.

ROUND 1

THE CHAMP

Oscar De La Hoya's impact on boxing was as swift as his flashing fists, as wondrous as that heart-melting smile. Undeniably, the U.S. Olympic gold medalist exudes a certain mystique possessed by few in the sport. De La Hoya's ring machismo is framed by smoldering sex appeal and an irresistible boyish charm. In the often-dark swamp that is boxing, he is a white swan. Or, if you believe all the hype, the next Sugar Ray Leonard. Whatever the case, the suave

welterweight champion grossed a reported $30 million his first four years.

De La Hoya's crossover appeal extends beyond boxing's crude, rudimentary underpinnings. Promoter Bob Arum understood from the beginning that the fighter's glamour and magnetism would pull in customers of all nationalities, but particularly the lucrative Hispanic and Latin pay-per-view television markets.

But for many Mexican nationals, the fighter's allure was muted by what they suspected was a reluctance to spill his blood — the blood of proud ancestors — if necessary. His Golden Boy moniker left

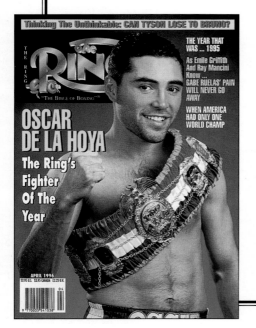

Before his January 1997 bout against Miguel Angel Gonzalez, Oscar guaranteed he would win using just his left hand. Although he worked in a few rights, the victory, combined with his outgoing personality, helped Oscar become boxing's favorite cover boy.

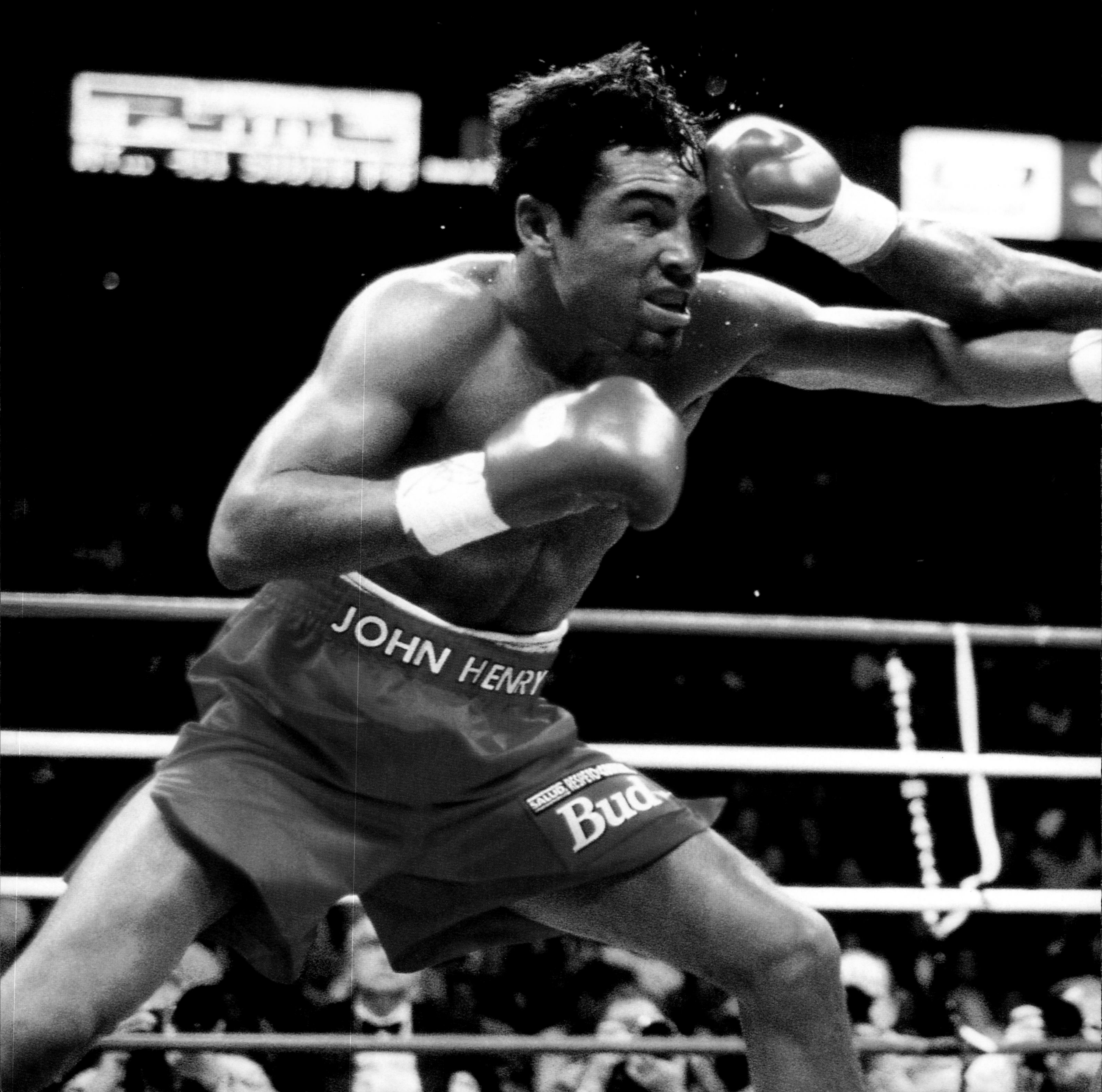
JOHN HENRY
Bud

them wary. Throngs of shrieking De La Hoya teen-age groupies needed just one long, lustful look to know they didn't care about such purist attitudes.

"I want to be a fighter who people say, 'Wow, he has it all,' " De La Hoya says.

A couple of titles and 21 victories in his first 3 1/2 years gave De La Hoya the springboard for the type of significant challenge he needed. First, he was faced with the task of attempting to conquer a monumental legend and an idol: Mexico's Julio Cesar Chavez.

When they fought in 1996, De La Hoya had just 21 professional fights; Chavez boasted 31 championship bouts alone. The untested challenger quickly sliced open a gash Chavez suffered

The 12-round victory by decision over Pernell Whitaker in April 1997 earned Oscar the WBC welterweight championship. Observers felt the win, in which De La Hoya seemed baffled by Whitaker's probing style, was closer than the scorecard indicated.

"HE FIGHTS LIKE A BAD GUY, BUT HE'S REALLY A GOOD GUY. HE HAS THE HEART OF A PRIZE FIGHTER. THERE HASN'T BEEN ANYONE LIKE HIM SINCE RAY LEONARD."

— LOU DIBELLA, HBO EXECUTIVE

Five months after the Whitaker fight, De La Hoya predicted he would knock out Hector Camacho. Though he relentlessly pounded the Macho man, Oscar settled for another 12-round decision and retained the WBC welterweight championship.

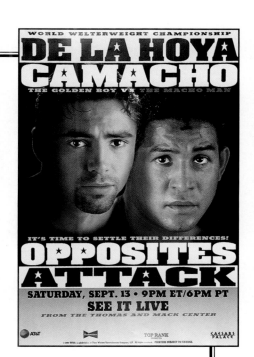

above his left eye during training, one he concealed before the fight. The faded junior welterweight champ's face was transformed into an angry blood mask. The fight was halted in the fourth round.

In an attempt to increase popularity with his target audience, De La Hoya defended his new 140-pound crown against Miguel Angel Gonzalez of Mexico. But the young champion's stamina was lacking. He settled for a 12-round decision and the embarrassment of a left eye swollen shut.

After two more wins by decision — over Pernell Whitaker and Hector Macho Camacho — De La Hoya had won his first 27 pro fights.

Boxing's Golden Boy had arrived.

ROUND 2

21

THE CONTENDER

On Nov. 23, 1992, dashing Oscar De La Hoya strolled into familiar surroundings, at least to his Mexican ancestry. The ballyhooed Golden Boy was about to make his professional debut at the Grand Olympic Auditorium in Inglewood, Calif., retracing the steps of his father and grandfather, who years earlier toiled at the revered boxing palace. Unlike the rough, battle-tested Mexican opponents his family prede-cessors confronted, De La Hoya would get a

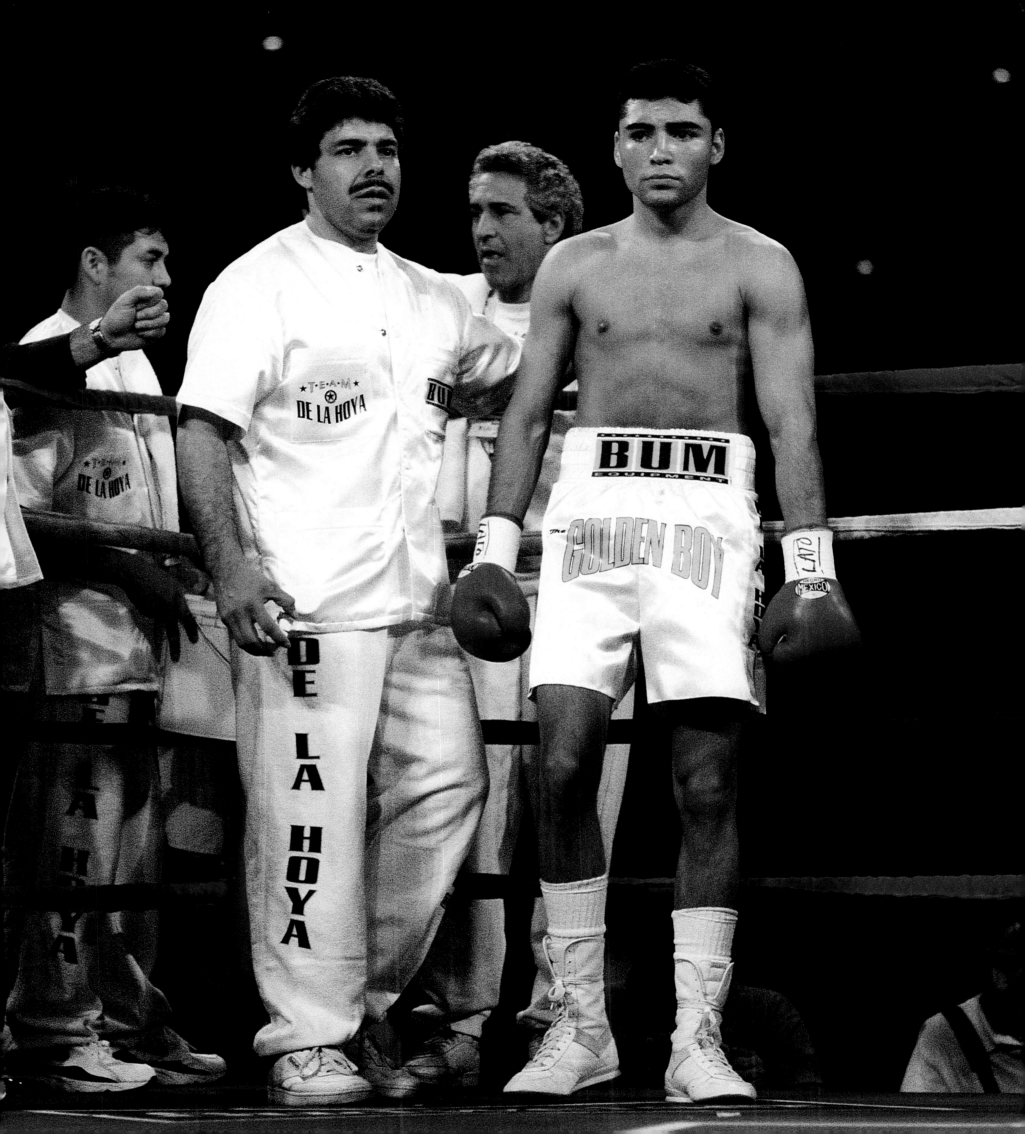

sucker for an opponent. Lamar Williams, freshly flown in from the shores of Lake Erie, turned out to be the catch of the day that De La Hoya's cagey management ordered. The budding star instantly hooked his lightweight chum with an assortment of lefts and whipping combinations. Three knockdowns later, all in the first round, the referee spared Williams further abuse.

Before long, boxing's boy wonder was battering opponents as if they were stationary piñatas. Less than a year after turning pro, De La Hoya carved out an 11-0 record. As if his superior height and reach advantage weren't overwhelming enough, his overmatched, shell-

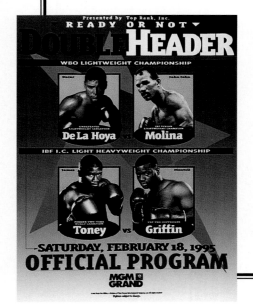

In 1994, Oscar dominated slippery southpaw Jimmi Bredahl to claim the WBO junior lightweight title. Programs from those early fights are now hot commodities among boxing collectors.

"HE HAS THE SAME SORT OF MOVEMENT, THE SAME SORT OF RHYTHM, AS SUGAR RAY ROBINSON. OSCAR MIGHT BE THE MOST NATURAL FIGHTER I'VE EVER TRAINED. HE COMES TO KNOCK YOUR BUTT OUT."

— TRAINER EMANUEL STEWARD

AN EARLY TITLE: 1994 WBO

LIGHTWEIGHT CHAMPIONSHIP.

Still, the champion-in-waiting was hardly a splashy LeRoy Neiman-like portrait of finished boxing art. On the ring canvas, De La Hoya was a work in progress. Nits were easy to pick: He was too robotic, too reliant on his natural power hand, shocked opponents needed radar to track his hand speed and reflexes.

the left; his defense was flawed, consisting mostly of standing erect and pulling back, arms outstretched. Two no-names popped a couple of bulbs on the De La Hoya marquee with flash knockdowns. His concerned managers gave him a new trainer — the fighter soon gave them the pink slip over finances.

Mini-controversies like that ignited media

brushfires, slightly scorching the boxer's cool, crafted image. But after just 14 fights, he captured championship belts at 130 and 135 pounds. In '94, Oscar won the WBO junior lightweight title. He added the WBO lightweight crown half a year later.

The enormous Golden Boy hype and pressure soon began to wear down the prodigy. By 1996, he not only looked ahead to the match against his idol, Mexican great Julio Cesar Chavez, but, curiously, also to "just getting away from boxing for a while."

Oscar successfully defended his WBO lightweight title in '95 against a quartet of former world champions: John-John Molina, Rafael Ruelas, Genaro Hernandez and Jesse James Leija.

ANATOMY OF A FIGHTER

Gil Clancy has spent most of his 75 years around boxers. He knows a good one when he sees one. When he looks at Oscar De La Hoya, he sees more than a boxer. He sees what in these days has become a rare commodity. "Oscar is a complete fighter," says Clancy, hired to help De La Hoya train before the Wilfredo Rivera bout in December 1997. "Not too many of them are [complete fighters] anymore, but he's well schooled already. He didn't get his record

OSCAR'S FIRST LINE OF OFFENSE:

THE LEFT JAB.

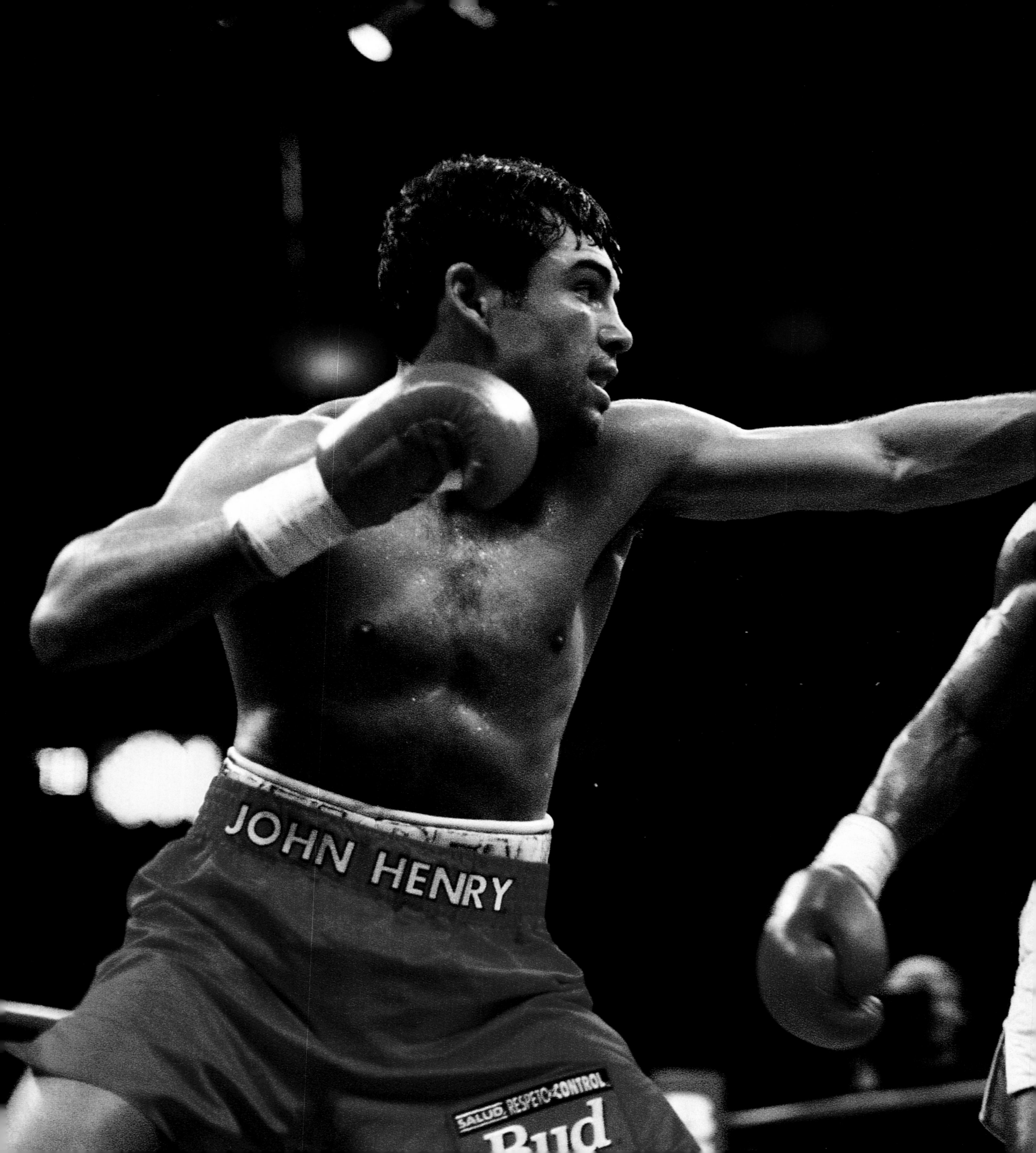
JOHN HENRY
Bud

Against distinguished veteran Pernell Whitaker, De La Hoya was hoping for a career-defining win but instead eked out a points victory. Soon after, his trainers altered Oscar's technique.

without being advised properly. He's complete."

There is little De La Hoya can't do in a boxing ring.

When he was fighting at junior lightweight, lightweight and junior welterweight, he was a freak of nature in the way Thomas Hearns once was. At 5-11 and 130 to 140 pounds, Oscar towered over his opponents, and his 72-inch reach gave him a great advantage over the much smaller men in his weight class. But as he moved up in class to win the welter-weight title, De La Hoya began to meet men his own size.

It didn't matter.

His left jab remained the same dominant

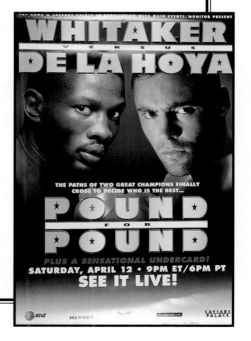

"I'M AN OFFENSIVE FIGHTER. IF I DON'T WORRY TOO MUCH ABOUT DEFENSE, I CAN KNOCK OUT ANYONE."

— OSCAR DE LA HOYA

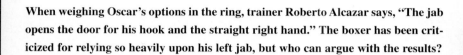

weapon it had been. Everything he does works off that jab, which can simply tear an opponent's defense apart. It is not a pawing, measuring stick, but rather like the picador's barbs in a bullfight. It is a weapon that does damage and softens up his opponents for what comes behind it: a powerful left hook and an only slightly less effective right hand.

Oscar has received some criticism for relying so heavily on his left hook and left jab, the same combination that broke down Julio Cesar Chavez. Admittedly, the right is the weakest weapon in his arsenal, but his straight right hand still hits with sufficient speed and power.

Unlike many fighters with his gifts, De La Hoya can also be patient in the ring. He tests his opponents to see how they react to his various attacks and then plots a way to set them up. He is an intelligent knockout machine who can overcome his frustrations and find a way to win on the rare nights he can't land his power shots.

Immediately out of the gate, Oscar attacks quickly and aggressively, barely giving his opponent room to breathe. Defense may be an afterthought, but his punches are like daggers, striking straight and true.

In the end, what more do you need?

43

ROUND 4

THE PUPIL

One could make the argument that Oscar De La Hoya is on an endless quest for perfection. "Maybe in three years or so, I'll give a perfect performance," De La Hoya said after his 27th straight victory, a pretty-close-to-perfect slicing and dicing of Wilfredo Rivera in December 1997. "And maybe not. Maybe I'll retire by then." But a by-product of De La Hoya's continuous charge toward flawlessness has been a bizarre game of musical chairs in his

"OSCAR GOES IN THE RING WITH THAT SWEET BABY FACE AND THEN ABOUT 45 SECONDS INTO THE FIGHT HE TURNS INTO A A STONE KILLER. THAT KID WANTS TO HURT YOU."

— TRAINER EMANUEL STEWARD

corner — he has been trained at various times by Carlos Ortiz, Roberto Alcazar, Jesus Rivero, Emanuel Steward and Gil Clancy.

Amid all the shuffling, Alcazar, a former fighter who befriended Oscar's father when they worked together in a Los Angeles factory, has remained a survivor. When Oscar first turned pro, Alcazar was deemed a novice trainer and was pushed aside in favor of Ortiz, a Hall of Fame lightweight in the late '50s known for his hell-bent style of fighting.

But De La Hoya did not take readily to the trainer's ultimate warrior philosophy, and Ortiz was quickly sent packing, setting the stage for Rivero, a professorish 67-year-old who had guided Miguel Canto to the

Even at age 6, Oscar was a willing pupil, proving both powerful and skilled in the ring. After his first medal, he says he immediately wanted another one. He ended up with 223 amateur victories.

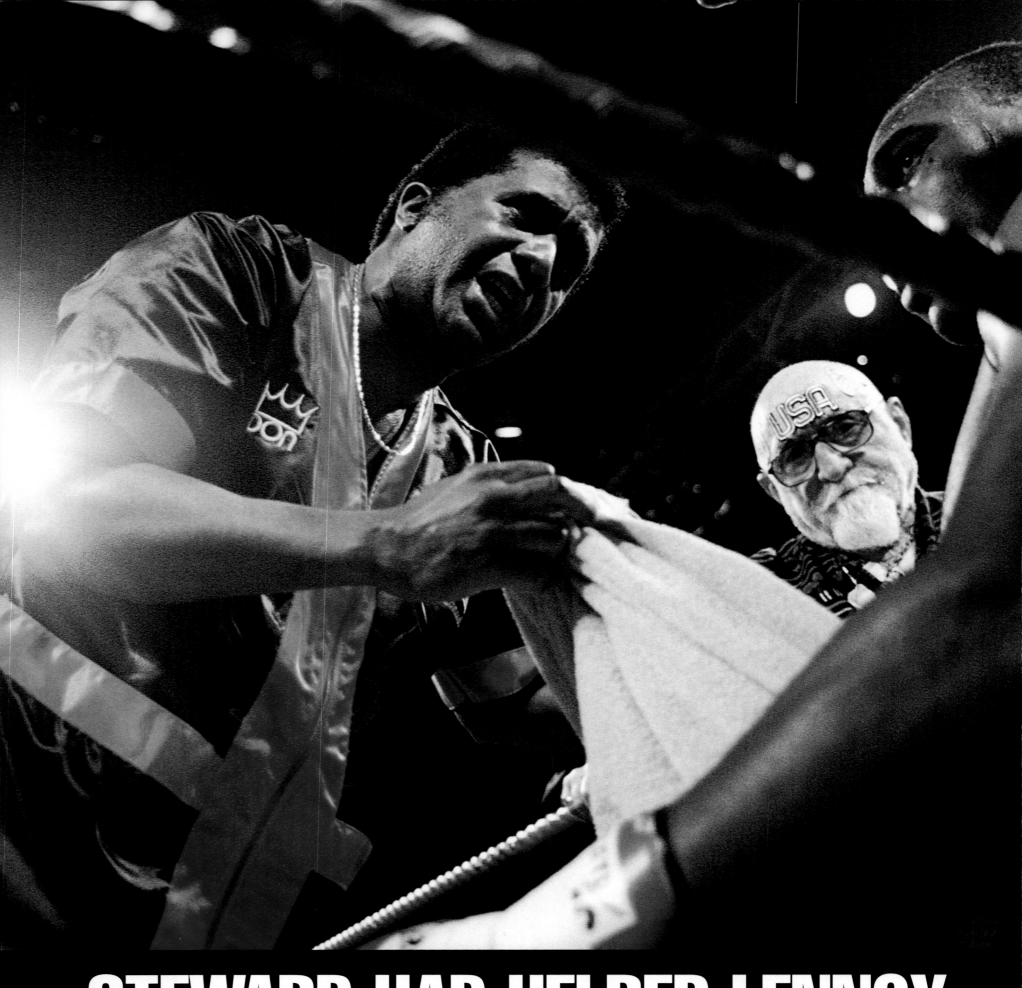

STEWARD HAD HELPED LENNOX,

BUT OSCAR OPTED FOR ALCAZAR.

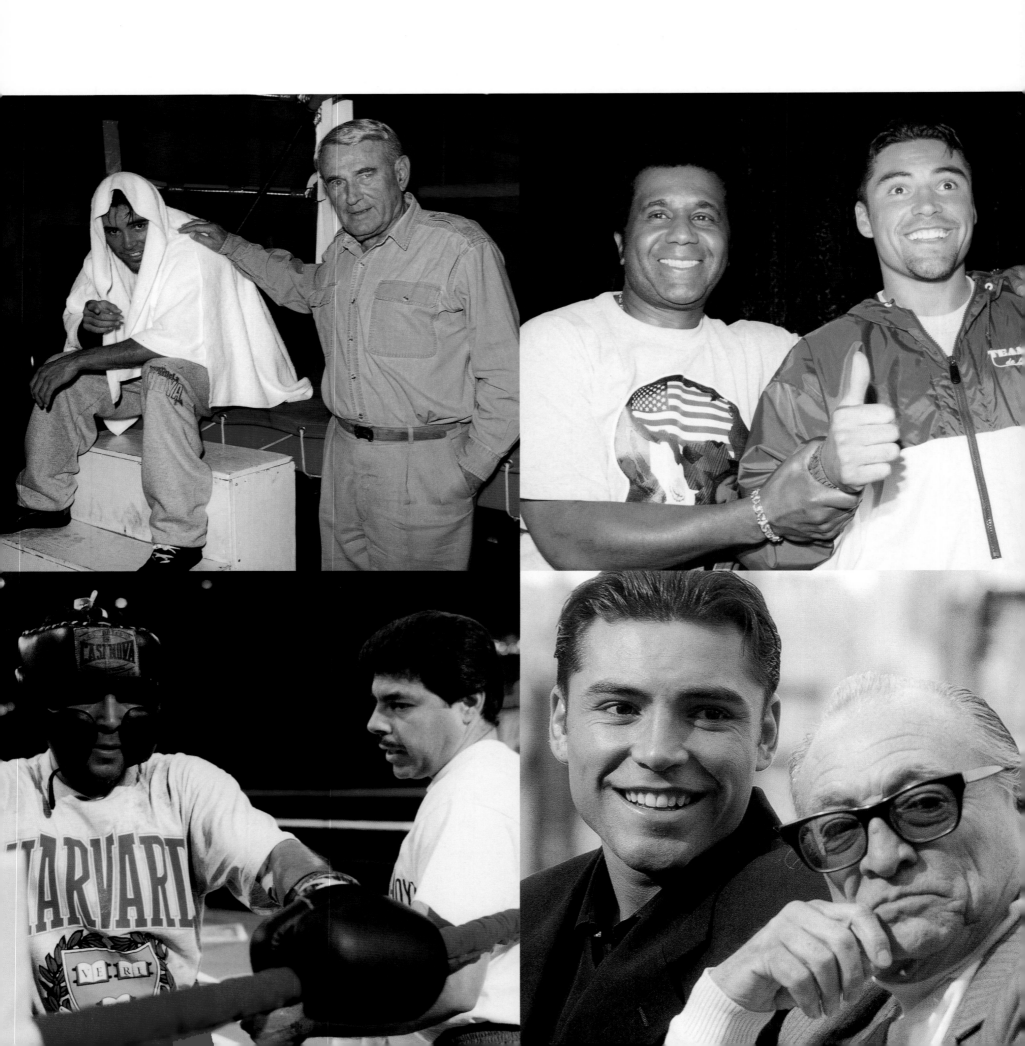

The procession of trainers has included (clockwise from top left) Gil Clancy, Emanuel Steward, Jesus Rivero and Roberto Alcazar. Ultimately, most of the changes were orchestrated by Oscar's father, with advisor Mike Hernandez, an L.A. car dealer, serving as mediator. It was Oscar's early success in the ring that earned him his own trading card.

flyweight crown. Rivero was recommended to Oscar by prominent agent Rafael Mendoza.

At first, it seemed like a marriage made in heaven. Rivero had De La Hoya read the classics and watch tapes of 1940s boxing master Willie Pep before Oscar destroyed fading legend Julio Cesar Chavez in four rounds in June 1996. But when Rivero began grabbing every microphone in sight, he was sent packing along with his complete set of Shakespeare.

De La Hoya next turned to Steward, a charismatic trainer best known for his lengthy relationship with Thomas Hearns but also credited with resurrecting the career of heavyweight champion Lennox Lewis.

Steward was expected to rekindle Oscar's aggressive nature after Rivero had stressed the art of defense. The immediate result was two seemingly flawless efforts: a knockout of David Kamau in April 1997 and then a complete domination of Hector Camacho in September '97. But Steward was soon dismissed, opening the door for Alcazar's return later that year.

To be sure, there were always circumstances and explanations to justify the constant changing of the guard, but some learned boxing figures believe the turmoil can do more harm down the road.

As the quest continues, so does the revolving door in Oscar's corner.

"It's like golf," says De La Hoya, himself a player with a 9 handicap. "If a teacher is not helping you, you get another one until your game is right or perfect. You have to keep improving."

ROUND 5

IN TRAINING

Oscar De La Hoya fought five times in 1997, unheard of for a world champion. Credit a strict training regimen. For each fight, De La Hoya trains a minimum of eight weeks at his private facility in Big Bear Lake, Calif. The busy fight schedule means there's little time spent in which Oscar's not preparing for a fight. In 1997, he trained a total of 40 weeks out of the year. "Every training camp that I have, it's just like starting over," De La Hoya says. "It's not like

Training at an altitude of 7,800 feet at Big Bear Lake, Calif., Oscar must put forth a little extra effort into his daily duties, which include two separate two-hour training sessions each day.

a to-be-continued training camp, where you start off your training like you finished your last training.

"What I do is, I train differently for every single fight. I change my style for every single fight, depending on my opponent."

Oscar hasn't always had his own gym, but he's trained somewhere in Big Bear since his professional debut in November 1992. His personal facility, furnished with a ring and weight room, wasn't completed until December 1995, just before he fought Jesse James Leija.

Outside the gym, among the pine trees, sits a large log home, an unattached log-covered sauna and picturesque grounds that include a sand trap and putting green.

61

"I WANT TO WORK
WITH HIS MIND.
I DON'T WANT TO MAKE
HIM A KILLER,
I WANT TO MAKE HIM
A HUMAN BEING."

— TRAINER JESUS RIVERO

Oscar normally trains in Big Bear, but during a couple of 1997 snowstorms, he found the going rough. "I was having trouble," he says, "finding a path to run in because of all the snow."

Before fighting Miguel Angel Gonzalez, Oscar violated one of boxing's oldest rules: No women in training camp. But Gonzalez came away awed by Oscar's boxing prowess. "He was a lot quicker than me," Miguel says. "I saw openings but I couldn't get my punches off. His jab is very fast and he would hit me with two or three shots and shake me up."

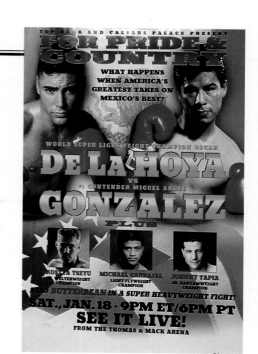

De La Hoya is a left-handed golfer, and a good one. "It relaxes me," he says.

De La Hoya may change his routine by sparring more rounds or doing more cardiovascular training for a specific opponent. But the more things change, the more some things stay the same.

O scar always runs at least five miles in the morning, followed by separate two-hour training sessions in the early afternoon and evening. Between the morning run and workout, he mostly naps. With his afternoon free time, he might hone his golf skills, or play pool or video games in his second-story bedroom. Sit-ups, heavy bag, speed bag, hand pads — they're all part of De La Hoya's routine.

Per tradition, there are certain distractions boxers had best avoid during training. De La Hoya vio-lated one of the oldest rules in the book before he defeated Miguel Angel Gonzalez in January 1997. Although Oscar won the fight easily on the score-cards, Gonzalez put a hurtin' on the Golden Boy, nearly closing his left eye.

"Now I know," Oscar says, "not to bring a girl-friend to training camp."

Before Oscar fought Rafael Ruelas, both fighters were training in the same California town. Problems arose when comments made by one boxer would get back to the other, and the De La Hoya camp quickly realized the need for a private training facility, hence the birth of Oscar's own training camp in Big Bear Lake, Calif.

ROUND 6

AMATEUR SUCCESS

On Aug. 8, 1992, Oscar De La Hoya's dream came true. The gold medal won at the Barcelona Olympics that day both fulfilled a promise and achieved a goal established many years before, thousands of miles away in the barrio of East Los Angeles. Oscar had dreamed of this golden moment ever since he was 6, when he first entered Resurrection Boxing Club on South Lorena Street in L.A. But, more importantly, the medal brought closure to a promise De La Hoya

A loss at the 1990 World Championships forced Oscar to change his fighting style, going more often to soft jabs to pile up electronic points instead of the more powerful, but not as productive, body blows. "People thought I lost something because I wasn't showing the same power," says Oscar, "but I was only there for one thing: to win the gold medal."

made to his mother before she died of breast cancer in 1990.

Cecilia De La Hoya had skipped radiation treatments to watch her son fight in the Goodwill Games earlier that year. She died at age 38. In the end, she asked only one thing of her son: that he win an Olympic gold medal. Oscar's plan was to leave Barcelona with the gold, and return the medal to his mother's grave site in Los Angeles.

"That is my motivation," De La Hoya admitted two weeks before the final tournament of his amateur career at Pavello Club Joventut de Badalona in a suburb of Barcelona. "To win the gold, it has to come from your heart."

The buildup to the Olympics was stressful and full of distractions. While turning his back on the street gangs that had infiltrated his neighborhood, De La Hoya skipped his senior prom to compete in a dual meet against Cuba in which he outpointed two-time world champion Julio Gonzales.

Then there was the sad saga of Al Stankie, Oscar's trainer who was suspended for three years by USA Boxing for showing up drunk during De La Hoya's victorious run through the 1990 National Championships in Colorado Springs, Colo. Eventually, the De La Hoya camp told the embattled trainer they'd had enough.

With all the setbacks, perhaps it shouldn't have been as shocking when De La Hoya lost at the World Championships in Sydney, Australia, to German Marco Rudolph — his first defeat in four years.

But through all the distractions, through all the

"THERE'S A LOT OF PRESSURE WHEN YOU'RE FAVORED TO **WIN THE GOLD.** SOME GUYS ARE COMING INTO THIS WITH NOTHING TO LOSE. **THE PRESSURE IS ON ME.**"
— OSCAR DE LA HOYA,
AT THE '92 OLYMPICS

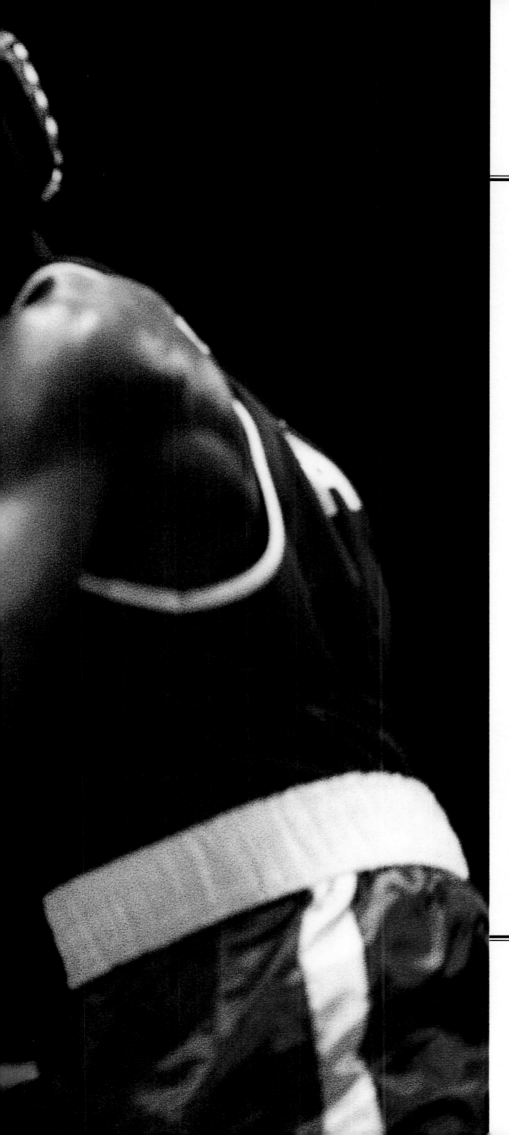

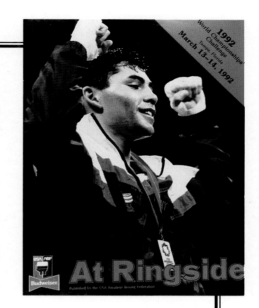

"Right away I thought about my mother," Oscar says of his golden Olympic moment. "She came to my mind when I raised my hand. She's looking down from the sky now and she's happy."

nightmares and disappointments, like all true champions Oscar bounced back. He became the only American boxing gold medalist at the '92 Olympic Games after claiming a 7-2 decision, fittingly enough, over Rudolph.

The cycle was complete. Oscar finished his amateur career with a record of 223-5. He had his gold medal, and he returned to L.A. and his mother's grave a conquering hero.

During his amateur career, Oscar got the chance to spar with his idol, Julio Cesar Chavez, who dropped the kid with a short right to the head. Years later, De La Hoya officially beat Chavez to win the WBC super lightweight championship.

OUTSIDE THE RING

When he isn't boxing, Oscar De La Hoya takes on an entirely different persona. Growing up in East L.A. under the watchful eye of his father, he developed a humble, humorous and polite personality. Now, when he's not managing the Oscar De La Hoya Foundation, he's winning over current boxing fans and attracting new ones.

ROUND 7

EL NIÑO

Oscar De La Hoya was not born to be a boxer. He was forged into a fighter by his father, as sure as a black-smith's hammering transforms iron into a sturdy tool. Joel De La Hoya would see to it that Oscar would not be devoured by the truancy, drug dealing and gang-land warfare that engulfed the barrios of crime-ridden East Los Angeles. Many people had an impact on the young boxer: family, friends, teachers, and of course, fighters like Paul Gonzalez, a fellow

Chicano homeboy from the hood who won an Olympic gold medal. But none had the lingering influence of Oscar's father, who arrived in the U.S. at age 16 from Durango, Mexico.

An ex-professional fighter of little distinction, Joel pounded away on his boy with relentless discipline and boxing instruction. In the gym and at home, it was the old man's way or the L.A. freeway. The boy considered him to be his best friend, and dealing with papa's forceful demeanor later gave Oscar a cool-under-fire presence able to handle pressure from all sources.

Joel tugged a pair of gloves over his 5-year-old son's tiny hands at the Resurrection Boys Club gym. Later, Oscar won his first tournament, halting a dazed oppo-

Little Oscar disdained physical confrontations with his peers. After he ran home crying enough, his father decided it was time to go to the gym for some boxing lessons.

"MY FATHER NEVER TELLS ME DIRECTLY WHAT TO DO. HE GIVES ME HIS OPINION. . . . I NEVER SAW MY FATHER CRY. HE'S NOT THE TYPE TO SHOW HIS EMOTIONS."

— OSCAR DE LA HOYA

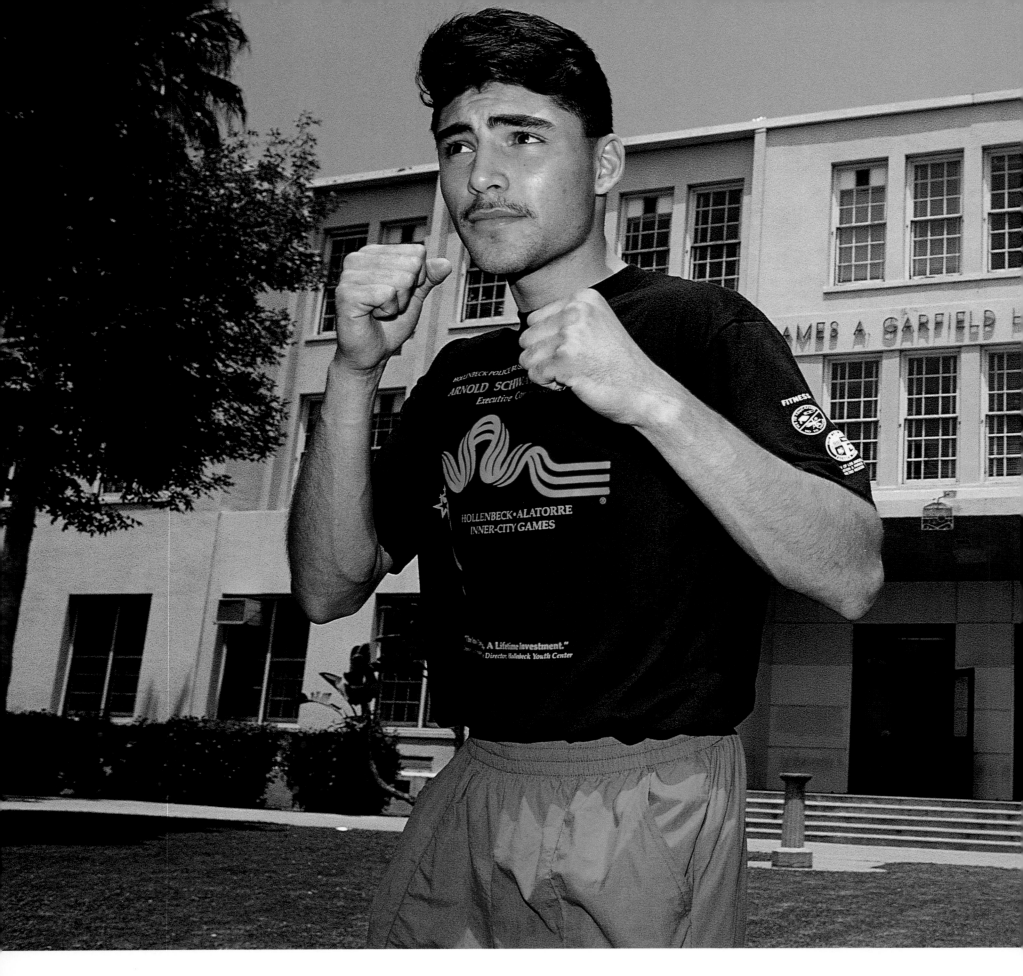

De La Hoya attended Garfield High, the school made famous by the film "Stand and Deliver." When Oscar needed advice, he often went to sister Cecilia, who was named after his mom.

nent in the first round. He was stunned when presented with a trophy, and smitten with the sport.

At 16, De La Hoya left Garfield High and studied with a private tutor. His dream was to study architecture at UCLA.

The love, support and spiritual blessings from Oscar's large, extended family provided him with a safety net from the dangers of his environment. The family often gathered at a festive restaurant owned by Oscar's grandfather, Vicente De La Hoya, to share meals, music and merriment.

Growing up in a tough neighborhood, Oscar dodged the dark forces that have fallen many youths. Out of all his victories, that stands as perhaps his greatest.

ROUND 8

CELEBRITY STATUS

In an age when the sports page often reads like the criminal court files, when even once-dignified stars act like spoiled, arrogant oafs, Oscar De La Hoya retains a humble, downright sweet disposition. His charming smile has become as familiar to the general public as the scowl of Mike Tyson. Oscar's quiet, polished demeanor outside the ring is complemented by his ferocity inside it. Walking softly and carrying a big punch, the Golden Boy clearly fears no one. He

No boxer can draw a crowd like Oscar De La Hoya. Among the celebs he's been spotted with: Sugar Ray Leonard, Sinbad, actor Mario López and Matthew McConaughey.

has fought some terribly tough men, all of them intent — almost desperate — to vanquish this stunning icon of an opponent. And Oscar has defeated every one.

But at the same time, he exudes a sort of kindness and humility. His image is that of the good guy in the white hat. It's remarkably desirable and marketable. And it is marketed carefully and profitably.

In 1997, his fifth year as a prizefighter, Oscar was the third-highest-paid athlete in the world ($38 million, including endorsements) behind just Michael Jordan ($78.3 million) and Evander Holyfield ($54.3 million). But in 1997, Jordan and Holyfield were well into their 30s. Oscar, at 24, was just getting started

and already the most marketable fighter in history. Meanwhile, the offers keep pouring in.

Oscar is the national spokesman for Anheuser-Busch's "Know When to Say When" campaign for responsible drinking. His milk mustache picture has been widely used among those of the many celebrities in the National Fluid Milk Processor Promotion Board's "Drink Milk" series. He can be seen in the trendiest of men's magazines modeling suave, sophisticated attire.

This is a world away from the experience of typical boxing champions who walk the streets unrecognized, bereft of endorsement offers. What sets Oscar apart? Something that can't be faked: charisma. His magnetic personality makes him a

OSCAR HELD HIS OWN

WITH JAY LENO.

Kurt Graetzer, an executive with the Food Milk Processor Education Board, calls Oscar "a humble person who is one of the best fighters of all time." De La Hoya is the only boxer featured in the popular "Got Milk?" milk mustache ads.

transcendent star. His popularity transcends the realm in which he excels.

The realm is boxing, but the essence of De La Hoya is something of a much larger scope. No matter how soft he walks, the punches remain big and strong. Oscar the fighter, Oscar the pitchman and Oscar the gentleman all add up to a breath of fresh air for the sport he plays.

For every endorsement he accepts, De La Hoya turns down about 10, says Integrated Sports International, a marketing firm that handles Oscar's corporate partnerships.

ROUND 9

HIS FANS

When Oscar De La Hoya faced off against an imposing Pernell Whitaker on April 12, 1997, in Las Vegas, the event drew a record 860,000 viewers, making it the highest grossing non-heavyweight fight in pay-per-view history. Bob Arum, De La Hoya's promoter, offers one reason for the sudden influx of fight game followers: women. "The extra interest Oscar has created — which no boxer in the 30 years I have been around has created, including Ali and Sugar Ray

Leonard — is his tremendous appeal to women, which is extraordinary," Arum explains.

For a boxer, it's virtually unheard of. We're not talking about some slick movie star or good-looking singer. We're talking about one of the most powerful all-around fighters in the world, the man The Ring magazine has dubbed the best fighter, pound-for-pound, out there.

Somehow, along with his sheer power and intimidation in a sport that has been, up to this point, reserved almost solely for males, De La Hoya has managed to package a unique charm, a surprising coolness, and perhaps a certain *je ne sais quoi* that's rare for his profession.

Oscar must keep security personnel around his training

With female fans securely in the fold, Oscar successfully wooed Hispanic males when word got out that he'd sunk $250,000 into renovating a gym in his old East L.A. neighborhood.

"IT'S VERY DIFFICULT AT TIMES [TO DEAL WITH THE MASSES OF FEMALE FANS]. BUT IT'S FUN. I'M NOT SAYING IT'S BAD. IT'S A GOOD PROBLEM TO HAVE, ACTUALLY."

— OSCAR DE LA HOYA

camp in Big Bear, Calif., 24 hours a day, mostly to stand guard against a possible onslaught of female fans. Night after night they plead with the guards for a glimpse of Oscar.

Las Vegas Review-Journal columnist John L. Smith notes that "when Oscar fights it's like a Beatles revival tour. The women do everything but throw their underwear into the ring."

Certainly, De La Hoya has that certain something that attracts people to a sport they normally wouldn't touch with a 10-foot pole.

"[People] who are not died-in-the-wool prizefight fans follow Oscar," notes Time Warner Sports president Seth Abraham, who has a vested interest in the pay-per-view world since Time Warner is HBO's parent company. "They are the people who came out for Ali, who came out for Tyson in his early years. Oscar's great appeal is he appeals to so many casual fans."

Somewhat surprisingly, the loyalty of Hispanics in general did not come easily. Many Latinos were indignant when the young Oscar dared to defeat their longtime hero, Julio Cesar Chavez. But as time and De La Hoya's many good deeds healed their hurt, Hispanics have found a new champion in Oscar.

And crossover star Oscar De La Hoya has now won over the most vital group of supporters a boxer can have: hard-core fight fans.

Using much more than his fists, Oscar sells tickets, pay-per-view subscriptions, deodorant, shoes, sportswear, shaving cream, milk, exercise videos, fan club memberships, his sport and, perhaps most importantly, himself.

HELPING OUT

Painted in mural form high atop the exterior of the Oscar De La Hoya Youth Boxing Center in East Los Angeles are the eyes of boxing's Golden Boy. Inside the eyes shine pictures of his gold medal and his mother, Cecilia, who died in 1991 from cancer. It's almost as if De La Hoya is holding watch on all the kids who enter his refurbished boxing club. It's a project he'll eventually duplicate across the country. The centers won't look identical, but they will be built

for the same reason — to help inner-city youths avoid the drugs, gangs and violence that have become all too alluring for kids who grow up under-privileged in a tough environment that demands a survival-of-the-fittest state of mind.

De La Hoya grew up in East L.A., home to arguably the toughest Mexican-American gangs in Southern California. He never was a gang member, but that doesn't mean growing up was a bowl of cherries. For some kids in the inner city, staying out of the gangs can be just as tough as belonging to one. The scrutiny can be daunting.

Hence, the birth of the Oscar De La Hoya Foundation. Its first project was the renovation of the 72-year-old Resurrection Gym. De La Hoya bought the gym

His work on Resurrection Gym having won back many Hispanic fans, a slew of celebs turned out for the Oscar De La Hoya Foundation charity dinner to see the host dressed for success.

113

"THANK YOU FOR REMINDING US THAT REPAIR OF THE WORLD DIDN'T DIE WITH ARTHUR ASHE."

— SETH ABRAHAM, CHIEF EXECUTIVE OFFICER

OF TIME WARNER SPORTS, SPEAKING TO OSCAR

Not many boxers could entice celebrities such as Magic Johnson and Jay Leno to show up at an event for charity, but both superstars found their way to the Oscar De La Hoya Foundation dinner.

in which he trained as a youth for $450,000 in May 1996. In September 1997, after Oscar spent another $500,000 for a major overhaul, the doors of the center reopened.

"Growing up in East L.A. and overcoming all the obstacles, it's very difficult," De La Hoya says. "All I want to do is help the kids."

Children are trained to box, and counselors give guidance and help with homework, constantly monitoring the kids' educational progress. It's all designed to build self-esteem, something De La Hoya says addicts and gangsters

lack. And this isn't your unfortunately ordinary, less-than-average community gym.

The floors, walls, locker room and equipment are all new. For boys and girls 18 and younger, it's all free. And with 150 members, the charity is thriving.

In December 1997, De La Hoya held the inaugural Evening with Champions benefit dinner and auction in Beverly Hills, Calif. He also speaks at elementary schools and visits children in hospitals. He believes nothing could be more important than helping youths.

"Kids are the future," De La Hoya says. "So let's open the door for them."

Built just after World War I, Resurrection Gym was originally a Catholic Church. De La Hoya spent nearly $1 million of his own money to buy and transform the building into a state-of-the-art practice facility for L.A. youth.

ROUND 11

ONE OF A KIND

Oscar De La Hoya has become a cross-cultural phenomenon, an American prize fighter of Mexican ancestry who is the hottest non-heavyweight draw in boxing since Sugar Ray Leonard still deserved to be called Sugar Ray. But what Oscar would really like to do is retire at 30 as a six-time world champion and then move on to other pursuits. Perhaps to architecture, which has been a passion of his for years and one he utilized when he designed

"I WANT TO USE MY IMAGE FOR GOOD THINGS. IT'S A BIG RESPONSIBILITY, BUT I WANT TO TAKE IT ON. BOXING NEEDS A CLEANER IMAGE."

— OSCAR DE LA HOYA

his home and training camp in Big Bear Lake, Calif., in the mountains above Los Angeles. Then again, perhaps it will be the movies. Acting is an idea he has toyed with from time to time, especially when a movie based on his life was under discussion.

What De La Hoya might do after boxing is hard to say, but he might not have to go any further than his beloved golf courses. When he took up golfing, De La Hoya became as obsessed with mastering it as he had with boxing. The more he played, the more some of his Hispanic fans resented their blue-collar hero taking up an activity typically reserved for the white-collar types.

Oscar is a celebrity superstar who happens to live in a city, L.A., that feeds off celebrity. He gets away from it all on the golf course with brother Joel and close friend Joe Pajar.

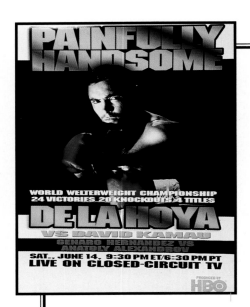

Oscar tried to understand, but he also refused to give up a passion he had developed for the most middle class of sports simply to suit someone else's image of what a fighter should be.

De La Hoya is all too familiar with the pitfalls of superstardom. It got to the point where he was spending $40,000 of his hard-earned money each month. When he realized his friends and family resented the new, free-wheeling Oscar, he changed.

"I decided I wanted to live a normal, regular life," he says. "You have to go back to the people and apologize, because I was losing my friends and my family. So I started apologizing."

128

In 1997, Oscar's handsome features and the you-have-to-see-it-to-believe-it hormonal rage that he inspires helped him earn $38 million, including $5 million in endorsements, second only to Evander Holyfield among boxers.

Then there was separation. Inside the ring Oscar is a killer. Outside of it he is a charming matinee idol.

"There has to be a difference between the street Oscar and the fighting Oscar," he says. "It's very strange, actually, the way my life is now. It's like a dream. I never thought I'd be in this position. It's amazing."

The Golden Boy image was left solely for the ring and the times his celebrity status was necessary to promote his work.

All the other times, he's simply Oscar.

ROUND 12

HIS LEGACY

Oscar De La Hoya is a man of many faces. For the cameras, advertisers and legion of teen-age female admirers, the barrio-graduate-turned-millionaire can be as charming and humble as the boy next door. But behind the beatific smile lurks a driven young warrior with a burning ambition. De La Hoya revels being named in the company of such boxing immortals as Sugar Ray Robinson and Willie Pep (at right), and his eyes light up at the mention of the more

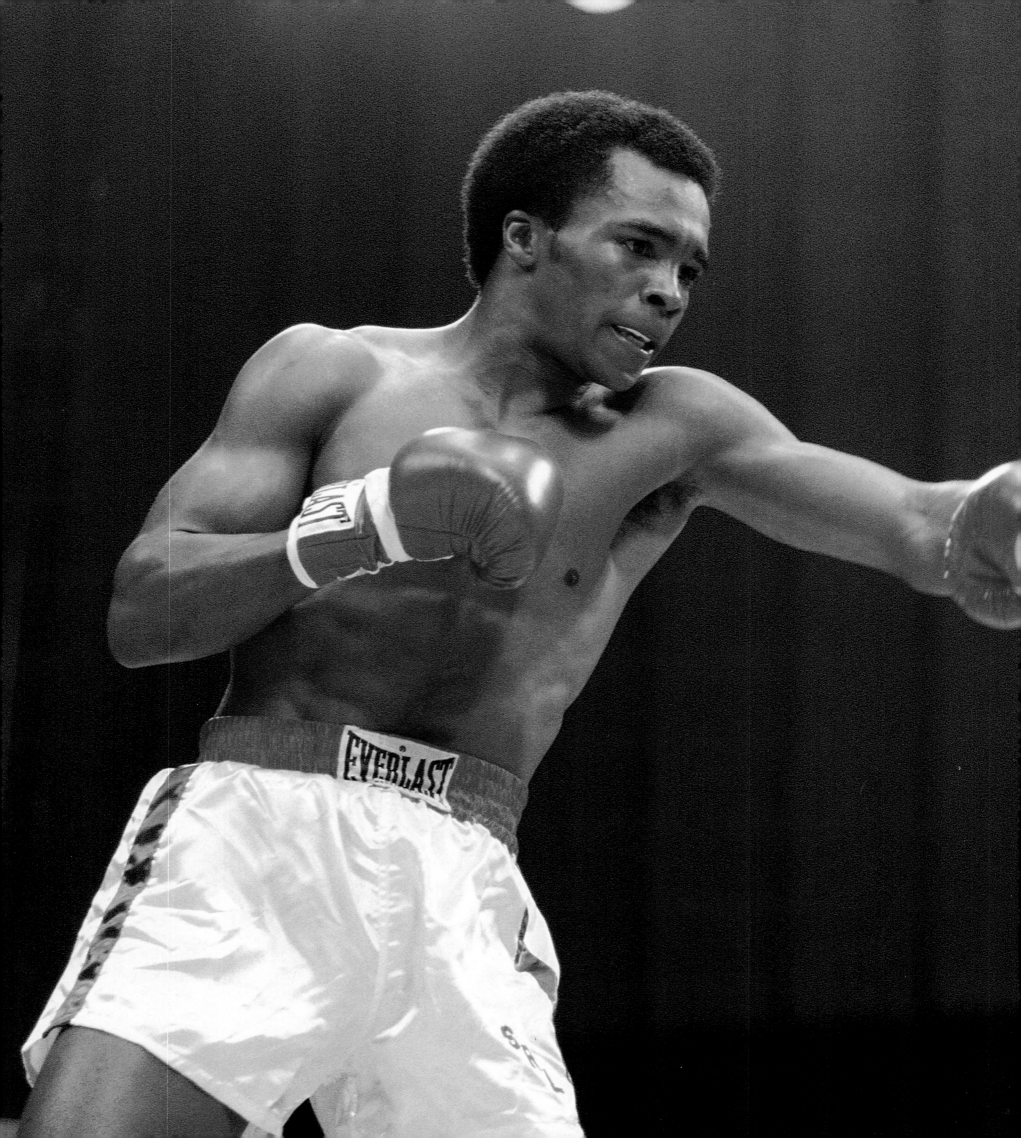

Ray Leonard is one fighter whom De La Hoya speaks of emulating at an early age (others include Alexis Arguello and Julio Cesar Chavez), but no boxer graces a cover like Oscar.

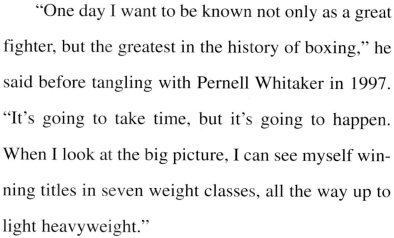

contemporary Sugar Ray Leonard. Indeed, on occasion, he sheds his humble public persona to reveal more desirous inner inklings.

"One day I want to be known not only as a great fighter, but the greatest in the history of boxing," he said before tangling with Pernell Whitaker in 1997. "It's going to take time, but it's going to happen. When I look at the big picture, I can see myself winning titles in seven weight classes, all the way up to light heavyweight."

Heady stuff, and in the opinion of some veteran ringsiders, a bit of a rush to judgment. To compare De La Hoya after 30-odd fights to the likes of a Robinson or Pep is, to many, almost sacrilegious.

"IF WE'RE PAINTING THE PERFECT PICTURE, OSCAR HAS TO BE FINISHED FIGHTING BY 29. OTHERWISE, IT WON'T BE PERFECT. YOU HANG AROUND TOO LONG, YOU'RE RICH, YOU GET OLD, BUT YOU ALSO GET BEATEN."

— PROMOTER BOB ARUM

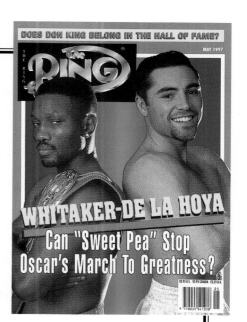

When they fought in April 1997, Pernell Whitaker was a distinguished veteran, a deft, confounding southpaw of indisputable merit, if a bit creaky at 33. He held a welterweight title and the additional prestige Oscar needed to bolster his ring resume.

In a sense, De La Hoya is caught between styles. Latin fans have criticized him for not being as macho as Julio Cesar Chavez, a fighter known as a relentless warrior willing to risk a bloody nose for the chance to land a solid punch of his own.

But that's not Oscar's modus operandi in the ring, as he proved in playing the matador while butchering Chavez in four rounds.

"I don't want to be just a gladiator," De La Hoya says. "I want to emulate boxers like Pep. I'm not going to apologize for not getting hit. And I'm not going to apologize for making my fights look too easy."

There's certainly something to be said for a

Oscar said of his big-time welterweight championship win over Whitaker, "I could have done 100 percent better in that fight. I was thinking too much. I should have been more aggressive."

fighter who makes winning routine and anything less than a knockout a disappointment, or for a fighter who had garnered world titles at 130, 135, 140 and 147 pounds by the time he turned 25.

Whatever face he puts forward, Oscar De La Hoya has the look of a champion.

"People say this kid is the best around," says promoter Bob Arum, who anointed De La Hoya as boxing's Golden Boy. "But when he ends up, a lot of people will say he was the best pound-for-pound fighter ever."

> By the time he turned 25, De La Hoya had world titles in four weight classes: 130, 135, 140 and 147 pounds. His goal? To retire at a relatively young age with championships in seven weight classes, all the way up to light heavyweight.

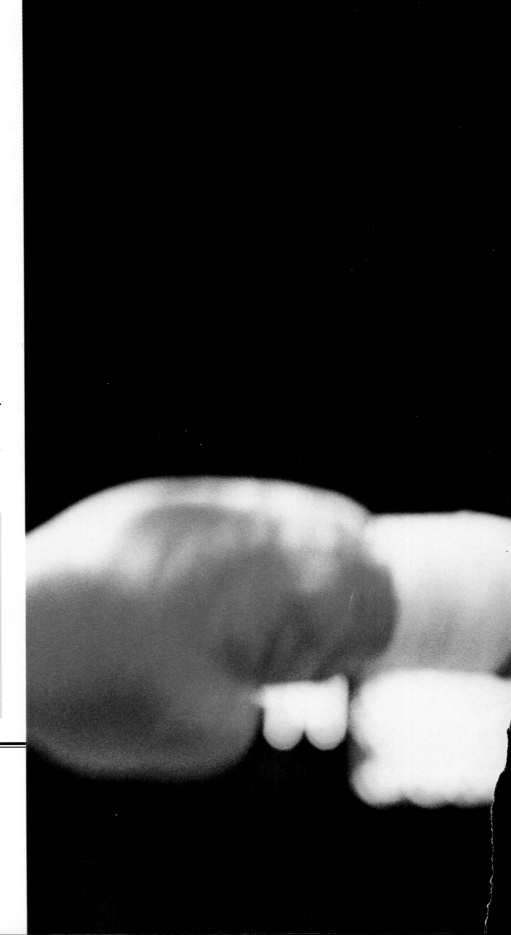

CONTRIBUTORS

Jon Saraceno is USA TODAY's Boxing Beat columnist and works as an analyst for ESPN.

Ron Borges covers boxing for The Boston Globe.

Alan Goldstein, the 1997 Boxing Writers Association Writer of the Year, covers boxing for The Baltimore Sun.

Robert Morales is the boxing columnist for the San Gabriel Valley Newspaper Group in Southern California.

Ivan Goldman, a freelance writer based in Long Beach, Calif., is the West Coast corespondent for The Ring magazine.

PHOTO CREDITS